The Dolphin

Illustrations: Marcelle Geneste
Text: Nadine Saunier

BARRON'S

New York • London • Toronto • Sydney

Dolphins always seem

to  .

They love to play around boats.
They slide to
the top of   .

Then they turn on their sides
or their backs and show
                    their white   .

Some of the words in this book are replaced by pictures.
These pictures reappear and are identified at the end of the book.

Dolphins breathe on the surface
of the water, like   .

They are mammals.
They have a spout on top of their heads;
through this small hole,

they  to each other in
high, sharp sounds.

In order to know what lies ahead,

or to  fish,

dolphins send
under the water,
up to 150,000 a second!

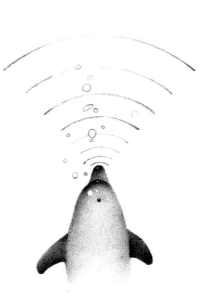

Sometimes
dolphins  themselves
on their tails,

and move backwards very quickly.

Their  are very powerful.

They move up and down,
not from side to side like fish.

Because of their smooth, shiny bodies, dolphins are able to

at a speed of
more than forty miles an hour.

Because their soft, gray skin is
very sensitive, dolphins must always

stay   .

Dolphins 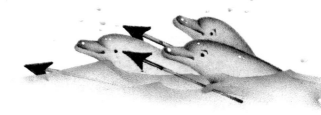 in groups.

They attack schools of sardines
or mackerel.

In order to avoid being cut by the fins
of   the dolphin

turns itself around. Then, with
its mouth, which looks like a

the dolphin swallows the fish head first.

Dolphins
mate by

in the water –

gently touching and biting and,
finally, resting their necks against each other.

One year later, a

is born.

The  dolphin is born tail first.

It weighs six to eight pounds.
It does not yet have
air in its lungs.
To keep it from drowning, its

and the other dolphins
quickly lift it up
to the   .

There! It is breathing.

Dolphins
that live in

in an aquarium

are able to learn many tricks.

They like people to

Like

and speak to them.
they are extremely
intelligent animals.

catch

stomach

beak

touch

tail

baby dolphin

pools

surface

waves

monkeys

balance

swim